FIND ᵣₙG ᵣHE WAY

Parables for a Secular Pilgrim

FINDING THE WAY

Parables for a Secular Pilgrim

Ben Whitney

A CIP catalogue record for this book is available from the British Library.

ISBN 978-0-9569568-1-1

Cover design by Clare Brayshaw

Prepared and printed by:

York Publishing Services Ltd
64 Hallfield Road
Layerthorpe
York YO31 7ZQ
Tel: 01904 431213

Website: www.yps-publishing.co.uk

Contents

About the author

Ben Whitney is a writer and freelance trainer, specialising in supporting schools in dealing with pastoral care and family issues. He is a former Baptist minister with a lifelong interest in the dialogue between Christian faith and our life in society. He is the author of a companion volume to this one: 'Walking without God', (Ben Whitney 2011, ISBN 978-0-9569568-0-4).

Introduction

A PRODIGAL SON

Hello again if you have walked along with me before; if not, where have you been? This is the second in a pair of short books in which I reflect on what is usually considered the province of 'proper' Christians, but starting from two conclusions that my life has led me to so far: (a) that there is no supernatural Being called 'God' and therefore no after-life to worry about, but (b) we each still have a responsibility to look critically within ourselves in order to be fully human.

My understanding of life is essentially rational and secular. Even if there were a God, it would be better for us to manage without relying on Him. We have to decide what happens, at least as far as we are able in a world that runs by natural processes, not under the control or even the influence of an external deity. But I am also in search of a 'humanist spirituality', if you like the term. A way of understanding myself that can do justice to the full depth of my humanity, but given that this is all there is.

Religious people are not alone in asking these deeper questions. I have learned a great deal from my son, for example, who is an academic philosopher and will soon be a brilliant teacher, even if I don't always understand him! This is a journey that has been undertaken by many people before – the search for truth about ourselves has been a constant part of human history. This is the same search, just starting from somewhere else other than a God. Again, I am not sure in advance where it will all lead. The journey itself is still the destination

In the first book, 'Walking Without God', I explored some of the big ideas of conventional religious faith through a re-interpretation of selected verses from the Psalms. These issues, such as suffering, loss, forgiveness and meaning, have to be addressed, even by secular humanists. I approached these questions with a genuine interest in the way the Judao/Christian religion in particular has dealt with them, but I had to do it differently as so many of the usual beliefs and doctrines simply do not accord with my experience. I meet more and more people these days who are prepared to say that they don't believe it all either, often after many years of church-going. I think we may still have something to say and deserve to be listened to.

This second book is much more about Jesus and re-visits some of the parables that were central to his teaching, at least according to three of the gospel writers. My interest is essentially in how we can best live together today, not primarily in historical or textual issues. So while I will at least try to understand the original context here and there, I don't feel tied to it. You won't need the Bible open as you read so that you can check my arguments against the actual words used, unless you're not already familiar with the stories. I am using them as a starting-point and in no way trying to expound their meaning verse by verse as others might do in a Bible study or sermon.

I will, of course, try not to put words into Jesus' mouth and be clear when it is me speaking, not him. But it's the new ideas that the parables might stimulate for my secular journey that I'm looking for. Many of them have had a significant influence on our wider cultural standards and beliefs, so are they of any use to people like me? Do they have a life beyond the believers? Deciding on the way to go can be complicated and stories often help us to make sense of things. I've even included one or two of my own to try and make things clearer.

Unlike some humanists I acknowledge that there is more to me than the purely physical, (though I do not believe I have an eternal 'soul'). A secular human life well-lived is still essentially about values and personal wholeness. However, churches, where the spirituality is centred around worship of a God, are difficult places to find much help. I seem to have no choice but to reject religious faith in the face of everything else that I know to be true. So I willingly accept my status as a prodigal, (I much prefer him anyway to the self-righteous older brother). But I want to appreciate the view from the 'faraway country' that I have reached so far and see where the signs will lead me next.

For those who have just joined in, I was raised as a Christian and for a short time I was even a Baptist minister as my father had been before me. That legacy is imprinted in who I am and I am grateful for it. There is much about it that gives me a framework within which to wrestle with these questions of universal significance. But, like everything else, what I have been told by others has to be questioned, not just assumed to be true. I am naturally suspicious of anyone who claims to 'know' what the truth is, beyond all discussion.

This book was kick-started into life by one of the worst sermons I have ever heard. Believe me, I've heard (and preached) a few contenders for that dubious honour! For a variety of reasons I occasionally suspend my disbelief and still attend Christian services, if largely as an observer. I especially appreciate the aesthetic beauty of the music in my local Cathedral, and I was recently present at a service for the ordination of deacons. The occasion was beautifully staged and enjoyable. But a senior figure in the Church of England could find absolutely nothing positive to say about the world beyond the church. The whole address could be summed up as 'There's a nasty secular world out there that has abandoned God and is interested only in itself; but at least we're alright Jack!'

You only have to look at the compassionate responses made by millions to 9/11, or to events like the famine in East Africa to know that this is utter nonsense. There is an enormous amount that is good in us, religious or not. It greatly depresses me that newly-ordained clergy are not being encouraged to look for it but rather to pull up the drawbridge and simply keep the faithful safe inside. There is no need for a God to explain our universal human capacity to care, to be hurt, to love. The idea that 'flesh' is bad but only 'spirit' is good is a dualistic invention we can easily do without. Why can we not just accept that our potential for goodness is part of our humanity, God or no God? Millions of others have come to same opinion and the church often appears to have no response other than 'you are wrong'.

Religion – all religion – is a human creation like any other, not somehow different or unique because a God is claimed to be involved. It can be done well, or badly, just like anything else. The Romans' and the Greeks' conviction that there was a whole panoply of rather entertaining supernatural Beings guiding their daily lives, is essentially the same as the claim that there is only one. It's not Christianity of course but it's recognisably the same kind of human activity, appropriate for their age and culture. Christian beliefs also come from a given historical time and place and reflect that context. But insights we have only discovered in the last two hundred years about the way the world is have moved the goalposts forever. Other views are now available.

All religions seek to make sense of our human experience – that is what they are for. As, in my view, there is no God who has sanctioned any one of them in particular, it is simply a question of which of these human formulations seems to have done the better job. Or perhaps we can now do as well without any of them. A God was taken for granted for centuries, but His existence is now rightly seen as a matter for individual decision, not as an indisputable fact. We each have to decide what is true for us. Like many others, I still have many beliefs about the way things are and how they should be; it's just that a supernatural God is not among them. That is not 'no faith'; it's just not a religious faith. Indeed a personal spirituality and value system that does not adhere to any particular religion might be seen as almost normal in our culture.

However, I am also stuck with my Christian roots and quite happy to accept them as an integral part of me. Others might have chosen art, literature, poetry or music as the framework for exploring these kinds of issues. Had I been born elsewhere I might have been raising the same questions about that religious tradition. So, while I accept that I am a runaway, I recognise that Christianity has had a significant influence on both me and the society around me which I can't entirely escape. So now I am turning to the parables in order continue my journey, and to the person who told them.

In my first book I was reluctant to refer to Jesus too much. Now I want to take him seriously, if (almost) entirely as an historical figure. Although I do not have his reference point of a God as my 'Father', there may be other points of contact which will resonate with my own experience and which can help me to find the way. He was a child of his time as I am child of mine, even if he was/is also the 'Son of God', whatever that phrase may have meant to him then or may mean to you now. But his humanity is a shared starting-point, though some believers effectively deny it, which is no more 'Christian' that I am.

I do not doubt that Jesus of Nazareth existed, (though his Hebrew name would have been closer to 'Joshua' than

'Jesus'). I also believe that at least some of his original teaching can be unravelled from what the church did with him afterwards. This may come as a welcome reassurance, though we cannot be sure we have ever got to the heart of the real historical Jesus because the only records we have to go on were written later by those who believed certain things about him. But it seems he was a wandering Jewish teacher who had some pretty radical views about the way things should be that eventually led to his execution. I have no problem with accepting any of that.

Neither do I dispute that Jesus came to understand his own life as a fulfilment of the ancient prophecies about the coming Messiah, though he was far from being alone in such a claim. Those of the Jewish faith say they are still waiting but perhaps the Messiah has been and gone and they have missed him – I don't know. Interestingly, given my travelling metaphor throughout both books, Christianity seems to have begun as sub-sect of Messianic Jews who were known simply as 'the people of the Way', not as a separate religion at all. However, it soon became clear that Jesus was not quite what was expected; something of a prodigal son himself who did not fulfil all the expected stereotypes and completely redefined the religious understandings of his time. This I like!

But I am very far from convinced by all the complex doctrines devised later that acclaimed him to be the 'Christ' for the whole world, not just for the Jews. ('Christ' is essentially from the Greek word for 'Messiah' but its meaning changes as a result of this wider application). A great edifice has been built upon the concept of 'the

Christ' which I genuinely do not think the actual human Jesus would recognise. It is as if there are two Jesuses; the real historical person and the object of faith — kept alive at first by those who knew him personally but then passed on from generation to generation. And, like Topsy, he has 'growed' along the way!

Over the centuries this Christ has been a King, an Emperor, a Victor, a Saviour, a Priest, a Superstar and much else besides. He has been used by some to exercise massive power and authority over others through wealthy and often intolerant organisations and structures. More and more beliefs about him, like the doctrine of the Trinity, had to be devised and then hotly debated as the church grew into new cultural settings, especially when it became the dominant political force in the western world. Once you equate Jesus of Nazareth with God Himself, a whole new set of questions arise requiring ever more complicated answers.

All this institutional complexity and religious dogma seems a very long way from the carpenter's son, (as the gospels suggest that Jesus was known), who upset the religious establishment of his day and whose death became a useful way for them to appease the Romans. Just another crucifixion among thousands. In my first book I suggested we could do without a God in order to be spiritual human beings. I guess I am now saying we can also do without the Christ that the church has created, but perhaps the baby should not be discarded along with the distinctly dirty bathwater. There is a real human Jesus behind it all. Maybe I am at least trying to be faithful to him as much as those who have turned him into a global brand which may not be true to what he intended to be. That's a big statement to make and I make it with some reluctance, but that's where I am.

So, to the parables. I cannot claim to be a Biblical scholar, though as any traveller should, I have at least done some research before I start out. When I was a child I was told that a parable was 'an earthly story with a heavenly meaning'. But that isn't true, just like the temperance lady who told me that the wine Jesus used at the Last Supper wasn't alcoholic, or my primary school teacher who insisted that the Bible was first written in Latin, whatever my father said! They're earthly stories with an earthly meaning – that's the whole point. They open us up, not to some other supernatural world, but to a hidden depth within this one. They demand an immediate response in the hearer and are often a direct challenge to way things are assumed to be, here and now.

The word 'parable' is the English form of the Greek word *parabole* which meant the putting of one thing alongside another by way of comparison or illustration. A parable is a simile or metaphor; a way of representing a truth by saying that it is like something else or by describing one thing as another. 'My love is like a red red rose' and 'life is not a bed of roses', are both parables. These are not statements to be taken literally; Robbie Burns' girlfriend did not actually have a red face and green spikes; life is not actually thought by anyone to be exactly like lying down on a pile of rose petals.

Images like these are designed to express a deeper truth by offering us a picture with which to enlarge our vision, not merely giving us a literal description. The parables offer an insight to reflect upon; they do not have to be factually accurate descriptions of real people or actual situations in order to do so. The Prodigal Son and the Good Samaritan may seem like real people. But they are just characters in a story, like Adam and Eve.

This way of story-telling probably also includes many of the characters from the earliest books in the Old Testament, like Abraham, Isaac and Jacob who should be seen as 'corporate personalities' representing great tribal movements and traditions, not necessarily as individuals. This idea is frequently found in ancient scriptures. Maybe even the concept of a 'God' is itself a parable – a human way to express the inexpressible, not a description of something that actually exists. There's a thought!

The parables of Jesus have sometimes been treated as allegories, like *Pilgrim's Progress,* in which each character in the story represents something else, but this is not the majority view. Some do seem to have particular allegorical elements but it would be a mistake to see every detail in this way as some early Christian writers suggested. The explanations that are sometimes given, such as the meaning of the types of seed in the parable of the sower, or Matthew's blatantly obvious addition to the story of the lost sheep, were added in later and reflect the life of the church at that point, not the pre-Christian time in which the story was first told.

Parables were not unique to Jesus. He may well have adapted some that were already in use. They were frequently used by the rabbis as a teaching method and there are plenty of other examples outside the Christian scriptures. Jesus would certainly have been aware of them. The Jewish people of his time also understood the concept of *mashal* in Hebrew; a brief sentence of popular wisdom or a proverb. This was a wider form of communication, of which there are many examples in the Old Testament, and with which Jesus would also have been very familiar.

However, if not unique to him, Jesus' parables seem to be highly typical of his teaching style. They are found extensively in the gospels of Matthew and Luke, together with a much smaller number in Mark. These three are usually referred to as the 'synoptic' gospels because they see things from a similar perspective. They have long been seen as a more authentic record of what Jesus might actually have said, compared with the much more subtlely-crafted and later gospel of John which has a very different purpose and from which the parables are almost entirely absent. They often contain a sting in the tail and can be scandalous in their implications. Some commentators think they were most likely told over a meal, with, as it were, an opportunity to continue the discussion over coffee!

There may also be a link to the Hebrew word *hidah* or riddle; statements that require some reflection before their meaning can be seen; pointers to a truth that require a little more work once the story is over. The effect might have been different on different people according to how they understood it. There may not always have been just one meaning. 'Let those with ears, hear' seems to have been a frequent ending. I like to think of Jesus' audience going home after supper and asking each other, 'What do you think he meant'? and not always coming to the same conclusion. A good sermon should do the same, not just give it all out on a plate with nothing left for the hearer to do. Signs point the way; they don't do the walking for you!

This apparent diversity in response is encouraging to people who start where I do. As with the Psalms I am not so worried about finding out exactly what the words meant at the time to those who first heard them. I am not even sure that such a thing is possible, though many of the stories seem to have a Messianic sub-text that fits their time of religious crisis. Jesus' sayings and teachings were only written down later by the gospel authors, not recorded *verbatim*. No doubt they were based on oral reminiscences from those who were there, but their original contexts had probably been long-forgotten. The same stories sometimes appear in different places so it seems they can have, as it were, more than one life.

Clearly, like everyone else, Jesus accepted the reality of a God and understood himself and his time in relation to that conviction. That will make some of the parables less accessible to me. But I doubt that will mean that Jesus' insights about life are of no value. So I plan to go on a little further than before, and I suspect there will be some new surprises along the way. That's what the parables should do – make you think about something from an entirely different angle and send you off in directions you hadn't anticipated. Again, you are more than welcome to join in. I only hope I can keep up!

1 Talents, treasures and hidden hoards

MATTHEW 25 VV.14-30; LUKE 19 VV.11-27

On the 5th July 2009, Terry Herbert was out metal-detecting, entirely legally, in a farmer's field about 3 miles away from where I live. Over the next five days he unearthed almost 250 bags of finds – over 1600 items altogether – many of them carefully-crafted examples of *cloisonné*: small objects made of incredibly delicate and detailed gold or silver with garnet inlays that need a magnifier to appreciate their full beauty. Very expensive, perhaps even royal; and it had all been buried there, just off the A5, since about the year 650!

One or two of the objects have religious connections: a folded cross that might have been used on a battlefield altar and a strip of gold bearing a warlike Latin inscription of Psalm 68 v.1, but they are mostly relics of weapons, stripped presumably from the losers. Why did it need to be so detailed? How did they make it when the naked eye can hardly see it? And some of the stones may have come from Sri Lanka – in the 7th century! (Sorry for being a Staffordshire hoard bore but we are very proud of it).

Quite why it was all put there and never retrieved is a mystery after all this time but, as Jesus shows here and elsewhere, burying precious things in the ground for safekeeping is nothing unusual. Samuel Pepys hid a parmesan cheese in his garden to protect it from the great fire of London in 1666. As with most precious discoveries, we often don't realise what is under our noses, and can easily miss them altogether. I drove within yards of this treasure every day on my way home from work without ever knowing it was there. To me the hoard speaks of the amazing potential that we humans have, and of how easy it is to ignore it or to lose it. But it may take some finding.

Discovery, from childhood onwards, is one of the most exciting features of being alive. Watching my grandson learn something new is a magical experience. Adults always need to be careful that that they don't lose its power to thrill and to amaze and settle only for what they know already. 'Become like little children'. Does that ring a bell? Not childish, that's different; but childlike. Like being ever-inquisitive and answering 'Why?' to every statement.

It is not only physical hoards of gold that we have found as mankind has come to know more about ourselves, our past, our world and even our universe. We are involved in a process of constant new discovery. Scientists are getting ever closer to finding a way to halt or even reverse the effects of muscular dystrophy, the muscle-wasting disease that killed my brother. What fantastic news that is! That's why I personally do not see the loss of faith in a God as a backward step. Like the fact that the earth goes round the sun – the church had trouble enough accepting that one – I see the questioning of the existence of God in our times as evidence of our growing human insight and understanding into the way things are. It is our world; and our responsibility to find out about it. Not a rebellion at all but a renaissance of our innate sense of enquiry that is a fundamental part of our true humanity.

So this has all set me thinking about Jesus' parable in a new way. Clearly the man who buried his rather meagre talent in the ground rather than make use of it, failed to set the example that Jesus was seeking to promote. Perhaps he felt he hadn't been given much so why bother? I wouldn't however argue, as some have done, that this parable proves that Jesus was therefore committed to the free operation of market forces and the values of capitalism! As I read it where I am today, the story is challenging me to make good use of the life I have been given; to be fully human because this is the only chance I am going to get. Not to bury my gifts and talents; (my pun, not his – it only works in translation), or live as if there is no more to be discovered, but to put what I have to work before it's too late.

My limited research suggests that this was one of many parables about the 'end time' which was on everyone's minds, (see, for example, chapter 8 about the very next story Matthew tells). It is one of a series of sayings about being ready for action in the coming crisis. It's not the man's lack of risk-taking that Jesus is criticising but his failure to do anything useful at all. It's another covert criticism of the religious elite who he saw as guardians of a treasure that they were wasting. For Jesus, sitting back in smug expectation was a failure to value God's gifts and a denial of Israel's responsibility to get ready for the coming crisis. It was talk like that of course which eventually led to his death.

So what treasures do I have and how should I use them? That's the question for the whole of this journey. We each have to decide how to live; there is no map, only a way. Along that way there are signs, from religion but also from elsewhere, and I carry in my backpack some things that may be useful. Of course, the pack can become a burden. We may be carrying things, especially from our past, that are best discarded. But the person I am is the main resource I have available and it's that which has to be used, not wasted.

When I consider Jesus' story I conclude that my treasures are my intellect, my loving relationships, my vision for the world, my experience, my compassion and so on. I may have 'gifts' in the more conventional sense but that seems to be largely a matter of luck, though maybe some of those, like playing the piano, would have become part of me if only I'd practised! Surely there's a lesson there. But these are the resources I personally have to draw on in order to get me through. Of course others will be different, but most of these are common to us all.

I have long been frustrated, for example, by the fact that so many people seem to leave their brains at the door when they go into a church. Loving God 'with all your mind' is supposed to be included. Most people are capable of much more thought than they realise; maybe it's laziness, maybe we're just all too busy. Too many seem just to want to be told what is true, not to find it out for themselves. But part of what makes us uniquely human is our ability to think; to reason. So why don't we use it more, rather than relying on methods of teaching and preaching which have decided what the right answers are in advance with little or no room for creative newness?

Our nation desperately needs people of vision, but they don't always fit the straitjackets that those who hold the strings of power want to impose. Compassion is not soft or weak; it is essential for our mutual wellbeing. And the treasure of relationships, in my case certainly, is something which may be hidden for some time but whose discovery brings enormous joy once we find it. This is the human story, unearthing hidden treasure as we go along, and how wonderfully exciting it can be. But it's up to us to get on with it, and then not to waste what we find.

An old man was leaning on his gate as a vicar walked by. 'That's a beautiful garden that you and the Almighty have created together', he said. 'Yes', replied the old man. 'You should have seen it when the Almighty had it all to Himself!' To go back to Jesus' slightly gardening-related story, if I am to discover what may be buried within and make proper use of it in the journey of life, the hard work will be down to me.

2 Mustard seeds, yeast (and a little bag of salt)

LUKE 13 VV.18-21; MATTHEW 13 VV.31-33;
MARK 4 VV.30-32

Just two chapters in and I already have a problem. Jesus began many of his sayings and teachings with the phrase 'The Kingdom of God is like this'. Short, pithy ones like these and much longer stories that go into great detail. I don't believe there is a God so am I lost before I've hardly started? It wouldn't be the first time. I have a pretty good sense of direction but not long ago I managed to walk through the same field of cows twice – and they weren't particularly friendly on either occasion. Or perhaps they were being over-friendly – I didn't wait to find out! But this already looks like a pretty significant obstacle in the way.

There is absolutely no disputing that 'the Kingdom of God' is central to everything that Jesus lived for, (though it's rather better translated as the 'rule' or the 'Kingship' of God to make it clear that it is not a place). He was not just some moral teacher who went about spouting helpful sayings: 'Drinka Pinta Milka Day'; 'Keep calm and carry on'. Much popular religious sentiment reduces him to little more than this. But this completely fails to reflect the drama of his life, or provide a reason for his death. Platitudes don't get you crucified.

At the beginning of his ministry in Nazareth, according at least some of the gospel accounts, Jesus identified himself with the one who would bring about that rule: 'The Spirit of the Lord is upon me, because he has chosen me to bring good news to the poor; freedom for the oppressed; sight to the blind and announce that the time has come'. Luke, ever the dramatist, says that he then rolled up the scroll, gave it back to the attendant and sat down. I bet you could have heard a pin drop, except for the sound of knives being sharpened. Most of Jesus' teaching is about the coming of the Kingdom. The parables are clearly designed to point to it, not least these little ones from the familiar worlds of farming and cooking.

A 'God' has been the way that most humans have defined their ultimate meaning throughout our history. But the overwhelming majority of people in our western culture no longer see the need for such an external explanation for the way things are, except perhaps occasionally at a superficial level. This simply reflects the new discoveries that I referred to in the previous chapter. What used to be assumed to be God's work has now been understood to be something else. There is no moral shame in such a position any more. Theists have to make their case, not act as if theirs is the only game in town. So how then am I to respond to Jesus' frequent talk of 'His' kingdom?

Jesus and the people of his time clearly took a God as given. I can't. No matter how much respect I have for him, there is nothing I can do about that. So I have to re-interpret his phrase if I am not to ignore him altogether. What he called 'the rule of God', I will have to call 'the world at its best', or even, 'life in all its fullness'. For me, you can take God away and you are left with exactly the same questions about how to live well. Or you can leave God in and you are left with exactly the same questions about how to live well! It's the living bit that matters, not the 'God' bit. Of course I am interested in what Jesus had to say. If he was right, these ways of living still apply, God or no God. The issues are unchanged by the change of understanding about where, or who, they come from. Because we're still here and we too have to work it out before it's all over and it's too late.

So let's get back to the kitchen. This right way to live isn't that obvious, then or now. It may need to be pointed out by those who have spent time looking for it. This too used to be the sole province of religious people but that's another thing that's changed – the people of God no longer have the monopoly on knowledge. But it may take a while to find the evidence we're looking for. Jesus uses of variety of images to suggest that what is right is often subtle, secret and gradual, but in the end powerful, uplifting and to the benefit of all. Small things can make a big difference. He is talking big numbers here; whole fields of mustard-seed and enough bread to feed 150 people.

It seems that Jesus is not interested in teaching the need for just a little bit of change that no-one will notice when it happens – this is transformation for the better on a grand scale, if from pretty insignificant beginnings.

Controversial for some perhaps; change can often be seen as a threat by those who like the way things are, as Jesus of course discovered. This is no recipe for a quiet life if we are to rise to his challenge (forgive me!)

At other places Jesus talks about how this growth in what is best may happen alongside what is not so good for us – the wheat and the weeds are muddled up together, at least this side of the final end to things. All this suggests to me that the right way to live is to look beyond the way things may apparently seem to be, and try to find the signs that something good is going on which is slowly but significantly changing the world for the better, often despite appearances to the contrary. And, I would stretch Jesus' similes just a little further and suggest that if it's going to happen, then, just as in the previous story, we will need to roll our sleeves up and do something to make it happen.

Seeds have to be planted and cared-for; dough has to be kneaded – both quite hard work. Again, these parables are not about sitting back while God gets on with it behind the scenes. This kingdom cannot be created without our active engagement. Encouraged by Jesus' stories, (if we want to be), we can at least believe that mustard seeds and yeast might not look much in themselves but, once set to work, they can have a powerful effect. Powerlessness is a quite understandable reaction if changing the world seems too much to handle, but for me there's no God out there to do it all for us.

So where to look for encouragement? How about Jesus' original manifesto? Are the poor receiving something for a change; are the blind recovering their sight and the oppressed being set free? The good news is that individuals are out there every day making a difference to the quality of human lives. And thanks to the miracle of Google they're not so hard to find these days. You can do the search for yourself of course but I like to keep an eye on the website of the Overseas Development Institute: www.developmentprogress.org/progress-stories. From progress in agriculture in Thailand to advancements in education and health in Rwanda; from improved political stability in El Salvador to increasing employment in India and the growth of democratic participation in at least parts of Africa, human beings are living at their best and making their communities a better place to be. Even a God could ask for no more.

To finish, here's another revisited parable to think about over a coffee. Jesus once used another kitchen item in a parable that consists of only seven words: 'You are like salt for all mankind' (Matthew 5 v.13 etc.). I only ever had one children's talk when I was briefly a Baptist minister but I could make it last 20 minutes if I had to! 'You know those crisps where the salt comes in a little bag? Well, they're rubbish. The crisps don't taste of salt at all'. (Much dramatic opening of crisp bag and eating of crisps – in church!). Small boy: 'That's because you haven't shaken the salt out of the bag, stupid!' 'Aaah, I see. Well that's a lot like life. Salt (you lot) isn't much use while it's safely inside the bag (the church). It has to be shaken out (dramatic actions) into the crisps (the world) and then it can make a difference.' (Much more mutual eating of crisps; 3 verses of 'One more step along the world I go' and home for lunch!).

3 Planks, splinters, houses and DIY morality

LUKE 6 VV.41-42 AND 46-49;
MATTHEW 7 VV.1-5 AND 24-27

Jesus was a carpenter. I gather the word used suggests a small-scale operation, probably making furniture and other items for the home, but he might also have had a hand in house-building. If there is a new religion around to rival the traditional ones these days, it's probably DIY and home improvement. You can't move for TV programmes on the subject and there will be more people in my local B and Q on a Sunday than will be in any church. Modern shopping centres even look a bit like Cathedrals.

So Jesus naturally uses carpentry and building images in these parables. First, be careful how you judge the behaviour of others. You might start picking at a splinter in someone else's eye while a plank is stuck in yours – not only obscuring your ability to see straight but also suggesting a bit of a double standard. And I've linked this idea to the story a few verses further on about the two house-builders. Like many of the parables, this one takes me right back to Sunday School. The wise man builds his house on rock; only the fool would build on sand. For a reason that I hope will become clearer, I'm going to think about these images in the opposite order.

One of the biggest challenges we face individually, and in communities, is deciding what moral standards to live by. (See chapter 7 for a discussion of a more social and political issue). We can't escape it. The knowledge of right and wrong in our human decision-making is the central issue in the story of the Garden of Eden. It is what makes us different from the animals. It offers us a chance of paradise but risks the complete opposite. What are the foundations of those values, or do we each just make them up for ourselves?

Christians, at least those of a certain kind, will usually tell me that the answers I seek are all to be found in the Bible. Of course Biblical standards have had a huge influence on our culture, as have other scriptures in other traditions. But it's not quite the knock-out argument that some maintain. Which bits of the Bible? – because it's not always consistent. And what about those issues that the Bible doesn't mention, including, for example, something as important as abortion or contraception? And where the issues are mentioned, like homosexuality, marriage and divorce, don't we now live in an entirely different culture where the assumptions made by people thousands of years ago can no longer be assumed to apply today? We wouldn't apply those standards to other areas of our contemporary life, like what to do if you are ill. We'll take all the modern medicines that are going then, not rely on the prescriptions of Leviticus. Much of the Bible inevitably feels totally out of place after all this time. It may be a rock for some; to me it feels more like sand – easily undermined.

OK then, so surely we can put our faith in the church; firmly built upon the rock, from St. Peter the Rock onwards? Well that worked for hundreds of years, but it doesn't work now, at least in our kind of open culture where a huge range of ideas compete for our attention. Even the church's own members don't necessarily follow all its teachings as they are supposed to. When the priest or vicar was the only educated man in the parish, and you'd better do what he said because your eternal destiny was at stake, maybe people more or less did as they were told – at least in public. It might seem easier to have someone else set the standards for you, but when they have to be applied to 'real' life they often fall apart. And, let's face it, the church has always had its own share of weaknesses. Its leaders are only human so can their advice be trusted? That also feels to me like sand. What used to be taken for granted now slips through our fingers.

'Well at least I can trust my own relationship with God and what He tells me to do'. I will be rather more cautious here because who am I to reject what someone else experiences as being true for them? I can only talk about what is true for me and a God does not come into it. But the fact that this 'revelation' is mediated though a human being – like all religious experiences by definition – makes it susceptible to being only what you have decided, not from 'God' at all. Claiming that 'God/Jesus has told me this is right' sounds very authoritative. But it doesn't actually have a very strong objective foundation beyond the individual concerned and risks taking me, at least, straight back to the beach.

Yet I do have more respect for this third approach than for the other two, (provided the person is sane and rational about it: 'God' has allegedly said all kinds of things to people which have turned out to be untrue or even utterly wrong). Because at least this person is accepting the decision that results as their own, even if they are relying on support from a higher authority as they have perceived it. But it's not just something they have looked up in a rule book or a result of the instruction of the church as if it's nothing to do with them.

If we do have a problem with our morality, and events like the 2011 street riots, for example, certainly suggest that at least some younger people in particular do, then it's not a lack of rules or guidance that's at fault. It's a failure to teach those involved personal responsibility and respect for themselves and others. In the end we each have to make a judgement about our own behaviour. No-one, nothing can do it for us. Threats of eventual punishment may have worked in the past, but not now. Saying they are God's standards doesn't matter much if we haven't made them our own. Those values might turn out to be built on rocks or sand; maybe we won't know at the time. But the only person I can trust to have thought about the issue and acted from the best of motives is me.

I must still allow the value to be challenged and tested, like the houses in Jesus' story. Some of my choices might then collapse under the pressure. But some will stand and prove to be reliable. I don't have to do this entirely alone; other people may have been there before. I can ask someone else what they think. That might help to make the value more secure. Or I might want to test out the likely effects of what I think is right. If it leads to a good outcome, then perhaps it's a good decision.

No doubt this all sounds a bit vague. But that's the way things are. Commandments only ever cover certain situations: 'Thou shalt not kill', except that there have always been plenty of exceptions when we do and it might even be necessary *in extremis*. A morality prescribed in the past may fail as soon as a new question comes along. How does relying on the Bible or the tradition of the church help us with nuclear power, stem cell research or assisted suicide? Certainly not by just checking the reference to what may have been true about something else in some other time and place as if that's an end to it. When push comes to shove we each have to take an existential leap of 'faith' – to put our trust in what we believe to be right, but then be prepared to change it if turns out to have consequences we hadn't anticipated.

Having said all that, Jesus might still be of some help, (as well as other people, of course, but he has centre stage here). So, back to planks and splinters. If there was one thing that seemed to anger him more than anything else it was hypocrisy – especially the hypocrisy of the religious. Casting stones at others should be the last thing on our minds when our own house is falling down around our ears. Lectures on the morality of others from church leaders, MPs or editors of newspapers have often been shown to have been built on the crumbliest of sand. Maybe the only word that matters in the end is 'integrity'. At least it has 'grit' at the heart of it!

4 An unexpected example – The Good Samaritan

LUKE 10 VV.25-37

'John was usually very cautious at the cash-machine, especially on these damp and gloomy evenings. He always made sure that no-one else could see his PIN and put the money away as quickly as he could. But this time he never even saw the muggers coming before he hit the ground. They took the cash, of course, as well as his wallet and mobile phone. There was no need to kick him while he was down as well, but at least they didn't stab him. He'd have given them what they wanted if they'd just asked for it.

It was quiet in the high street tonight. Not many people about and those that were there were obviously anxious to get home. The vicar was no doubt too pre-occupied to notice him, hurrying to get to Evensong after a particularly trying pastoral visit. The police patrol car didn't even slow down; probably going to some other emergency of greater importance. The doctor's surgery across the road was, inevitably, closed.

It was getting dark now. His ribs were beginning to hurt even more. So John was worried at first when the unlicensed minicab stopped and this young Asian chap got out. Hadn't he suffered enough already? John had never been too keen on 'Pakis'. What with their foreign ways and their funny food: why didn't they go back where they came from? He was even more surprised when the driver asked him if he was alright, then gently led him to his car and took him to Casualty. He even bought him a cup of tea and stayed with him till John's daughter arrived. 'No charge mate', he said, as he left. John never did get his name. So who was the good guy here? It's a no-brainer!'

It's a timeless story and let's not worry too much about whether Jesus actually told it himself just as it stands. It's consistent with his teaching elsewhere. It's such a powerful image that it is odd that none of the other gospels included it; usually there's quite a bit of overlap, so the general assumption is that Mark and Matthew didn't know about it. Luke may well have had access to sources not available to the earliest writers so let's settle for that.

The context within which the story is set is important this time. Jesus had been asked a question by some smart-ass religious lawyer about what he must do to receive eternal life. Of course he thought he knew the answer to his own question already. Follow the law; keep the commandments and so on. Presumably this was some kind of trap for Jesus to fall into and to see how well this so-called teacher knew his stuff. But, like all good interviewees, Jesus answers the question with another question – 'What do the scriptures say? How do you read them?' The lawyer comes back with the standard formula about loving both God and neighbour. Job done.

Jesus didn't get into a discussion about God. I suppose that part was assumed. 'So love your neighbour then' he says. 'Ah, but who is my neighbour'? Not quite who he thought he was, as the story then makes clear. The Jews loathed and despised the Samaritans. They were the inheritors of the renegade tribes which had split from the true nation centuries before. Samaritans were outsiders, lesser people, who did not enjoy God's favour. And it was one of these who Jesus holds up as the example for the lawyer to follow. I bet he went off muttering a few choice non-legal words under his breath!

This is not just a story just about doing good works though it is partly about that of course. If I am looking for signposts about how to live well, then the example of the Good Samaritan is obviously one of them. Over the years it has inspired both religious and non-religious people alike to make the world a better place, and where would we all be now without them? Chad Varah, the priest who founded the modern-day Samaritans, set the organisation up because he heard of a young girl who had killed herself because she had started menstruating. Because she didn't understand what was happening to her, she assumed she must be suffering from some dreadful disease and, it seems, she had no-one to turn to for help. So he set up a few phone lines and recruited a few volunteers to be on hand so that there was someone the suicidal and the desperate could turn to.

But there's another dimension to the story that seems to have been Jesus' real point. This isn't a story about a Jew helping a Samaritan – commendable and exemplary as that would have been for the lawyer to follow. It's a story about a Samaritan helping a Jew; about the outsider being held up as an example. It's about breaking down prejudice and recognising that there is goodness to be found in some very unlikely places. It's about allowing others to do good to us and recognising their value as an example, even if they are not 'one of us'. The same idea can be found elsewhere when Jesus talks about loving your enemies, blessing those who curse you and doing good to those who hate you. Loving your friends is easy. Jesus seems to be expecting rather more.

This is why I get so cross when those who do believe in God seem to assume that they are somehow morally superior to those of us who do not. Jesus takes the very opposite view. The faithful might need to learn a lesson from the faithless. It is not enough just to do good to those who are close to us; those like us; those with whom we are already on friendly terms and who would no doubt do the same for us. The model of the Good Samaritan is that he did good to someone from whom he was estranged, who thought he was beneath him and who might not have given him the time of day had the roles been reversed. The man who was robbed might not have 'deserved' the help he got, but it was offered anyway. Would the Jew have stopped for the Samaritan? Would John have come to the rescue of the taxi-driver? Would the Protestant necessarily help the Catholic or the Christian stand up for the atheist? Maybe not. The example being set is much more than might at first appear.

I may not believe that there is a God but I do discern a pretty superhuman standard here by which I would like to live. In 'Walking without God' I wrote about our tendency to divide people into 'goodies' and baddies'. Individuals, societies and religions all do much the same. Of course there are genuine victims out there who are entitled to our sympathy and support; people who have been appallingly treated and ill-used. As I write, the case of the murder of schoolgirl Millie Dowler is in the news again. How dreadfully that family has suffered and not just at the hands of the man who killed their daughter. How much they deserve our heartfelt compassion. They have every right not to be overlooked and that may seem challenging enough.

But some of those who most need our compassion might not seem to deserve it quite so much, and might not have shown it to us had we been in need of help from them. Yet they should get it anyway. There's an old joke about the social worker who, on hearing the story about the Good Samaritan, remarked that the robbers obviously needed help! The Samaritan could have passed by on the moral high ground and no-one from either community would have thought any the worse of him as a result. He chose not to do so and Jesus holds him up as an unexpected example to those who were pretty sure they knew who was good and who was not. That seems to me like an even bigger challenge and it gives me plenty more to think about along the way.

5 True happiness – The Beatitudes

MATTHEW 5 VV.1-12; LUKE 6 VV.20-23

It's my book so I can break my own rules if I want to, like a non-scoring round in the middle of a quiz on Radio 4! We are much closer here to *mashal* or *hidah* than *parabole*, but it would seem unwise to leave out the place where Jesus talks so explicitly about how to live. This series of sayings has been placed by the gospel writers as the beginning to what we call the 'Sermon on the Mount'. The versions are not quite the same, (and Luke says that he came down from the hill to a 'level place' first, not up it), and they might have been spoken on different occasions, not actually in one address, but that's all by the by.

I'm afraid that people of my generation who have not always conformed to what good Christians might expect, immediately think of 'The Life of Brian'. There were parts of that film that I didn't think worked, especially the ending, but it was only ever meant to be a send-up of religious films, not to insult Jesus himself. Let's face it, those films deserved it. There was a time when there was nothing else to do on Good Friday except go to the cinema and sit through them. There's a no doubt apocryphal story about John Wayne, who played the centurion at the foot of the cross in one of the worst. He only had one line:

'Truly this was the Son of God!' The director asked him to say it with more reverence, more awe. 'Aaaaw terruly this was the Son of Gaard!' was all he got!

But the people at the back struggling to hear in 'The Life of Brian' and the confusion over the blessedness of the 'cheesemakers' did make me laugh. It captured the idea of the little people in life finding something in what Jesus said to encourage them to feel better about themselves, and that's the theme I want to pursue. The Good News Bible, interestingly, settles for 'happiness' as the translation, not 'blessed' as in most versions. 'Blessed' implies the well-being comes from Someone else; 'happy' just brings to mind the state of mind that everyone would like to have, religious or not.

We are said not to be very happy with our lives in 21st century Britain. The suicide rate has been rising, as it inevitably does during times of economic recession. More worryingly, ever younger people seem to be taking their own lives including, as I know from my own professional work, even children and teenagers. Politicians have become something of a laughing-stock for trying to create a 'wellbeing' index to measure our happiness, but I can see what they are trying to do. It will be a great pity if schools no longer have the time to focus on the social and emotional aspects of growing up as well as on academic learning. Our young people need to be taught how to deal with what life will throw at them, no matter how clever they are.

But we ought to have everything going for us. We are still in the top ten richest nations in the world. Most of us have a standard of living way above what is normal in two-thirds of countries elsewhere. Unemployment is a scourge, but most of us still have a job, if not one that necessarily gives us much dignity. Too many people are stuck in relative poverty but at least there is usually hope of some improvement or other ways to make life worthwhile. Most people still believe in falling in love and hope for happiness in their personal relationships, even if things don't always work out that way.

However, it seems that many have lost their capacity to cope with inevitable disappointments; what my mother would have called 'stickability' and what the psychologists might now call 'resilience'. I spent most of my career, once I stopped being a minister, trying to encourage teenagers to go to school, and nagging their parents to take more responsibility for making sure they did. I wasn't all that successful most of the time. They gave up so easily. The slightest barrier in their way, the merest hint of a problem that might have to be overcome first and that was it. For years, I had a picture on my desk, drawn by my daughter when she was little. It showed Miffy the Rabbit, looking glum because another rabbit had just taken her balloon. The caption, and neither of us know how it came to be there, said 'Life is not easy!' How true.

At this point, Jesus' teaching seems to be a message of hope about how to be resilient in a far from easy life. It can simply be seen as saying that those who are having a hard time of it now will receive their compensation in some future existence. That's a reassuring thought to many, though the reward seems to be available pretty generally according to Jesus, not tied up with strings that bind you to particular religious beliefs first. This is not the only place where Jesus seems to be suggesting that the grace of his God is rather more generous and universal than God so often appears to be. (I was disappointed, though not entirely surprised, to see that a book from the evangelical tradition suggesting such a thing has been banned by several 'Christian' bookshops).

My emphasis, of course, cannot be on an after-life, but on this one. The danger of that version of the 'compensation culture' is that it can lead us to think there's no need to take account of the poor, the humble etc. this side of eternity. They will have their reward then so should just wait for it patiently. But it seems to me that Jesus is also saying that these are the kinds of values that really matter and which, despite all appearances, do actually offer the best possibility of true human happiness. We should take more notice of them here and now if we want to know how to live. This is not just saying 'Always look on the bright side of life'! It is about recognising the true potential within our given circumstances and that true happiness, true blessedness, is still within our grasp, despite how it will often feel.

Life can be hard, even in our privileged culture. Jesus does not say that happiness lies in avoiding all such negative experiences. 'How happy are those who never have any problems in life and who sail through on a cloud of niceness!' I don't think so. But if we have come to a full knowledge of ourselves, then we will find the resilience to handle the difficulties that being human inevitably brings.

Even the spiritually poor can still find the rule of God, or, as I would put it, be a part of the world at its best:

Happy are those who mourn, because only those who have never loved can hope to never be sad.

Happy are those who are humble, because they will also find joy in the happiness of others, not only in their own.

Happy are those who try to live life to the very best of their potential; they will find something good in every experience.

Happy are those who are merciful because they will then be able to enjoy the forgiveness of others when they need it.

Happy are the pure in heart; for they know that goodness is real and see it more easily than those who are bitter.

Happy are those who work for peace because they will experience the joy of seeing others reconciled.

Happy are those who are persecuted because, even if the way is hard, knowing you have been true to yourself is actually all that matters.

6 Sheep, shepherds and 'Trespassers welcome'

LUKE 15 VV.1-7; MATTHEW 18 VV. 10-14

There's an awful lot about sheep in the gospels. They were a familiar sight to Jesus' audience of course, and you still see them in their hundreds on most country walks. These days they all seem to have numbers on their backs like bingo balls. In the Mountains of Mourne in Northern Ireland I have even seen Protestant sheep and Catholic sheep, marked either with red, white and blue or green!

The metaphor of Jesus as a shepherd crops up repeatedly, not least in John 10. John may not include many parables but he has almost a whole chapter on Jesus as the Good Shepherd. It's a touching image that has gone deep into our thinking. It has given us the word 'pastoral' in schools as well as churches. When I was a minister, my colleagues used to talk about 'sheep stealing'. As it was a brewery town I was bit confused at first but they meant people who were pinched from one church by another! I'm not sure it's all that flattering for Christians to be compared with sheep but there we are. This chapter is about the church, though it might be thought I'm in no position to comment.

As pretty much an outsider these days I do have to tread carefully here. A young man was driving his sports car along a country lane when he stopped to speak to a shepherd. 'If I can tell you how many sheep you've got in that field, can I take one away?' 'Sure' the shepherd replied. So the guy got out his Blackberry, downloaded a GPS image of the field and ran it through his laptop. '186', he said. 'Dead right', said the shepherd and the man put one of the animals into the boot. 'Hang on', said the shepherd. 'If I can tell you what job you do, can I have it back'? 'Sure, said the young man. 'You're one of them consultants aren't you'? 'How did you know that'? 'Well', said the shepherd; 'You turned up here even though you weren't invited. You had the cheek to want paying for telling me something I already knew. And you obviously don't know the first thing about my business. Now, can I have my dog back'!?

But maybe an external eye is useful now and again. What is the Christian church for these days and do you have to attend its worship or even believe in its God to live a 'Christian' life? The second leg of this journey began with my frustration at a poor piece of preaching that was little more than a bit of mutual back-slapping. That can't be enough. It seemed easier to know what the church was for in the past when the churches, especially the Church of England ran everything. There are still relics of this idea around of course. It is very hard to imagine a royal wedding that isn't a church service and even most politicians still seem to want to portray themselves as at least nominal Christians, notwithstanding Alistair

Campbell's reluctance for Tony Blair to 'do God'. The church still exercises considerable power over people's lives.

But I wonder what percentage of people in their parish church on a Sunday morning, Protestant or Catholic, are only there because they want to get their child into the 'best' local school or to get married in a picturesque setting? I don't blame them; it's a game that you just have to play. I also wonder what on earth they make of it all. Does it have anything to do with the rest of their lives? It was Archbishop William Temple who said that the church was the only organisation that existed for the benefit of those who were not its members. Jesus' story of the shepherd going out to look for the one sheep that was lost, especially in Luke's version, suggests that it's the outsiders that really mattered to him. The 99 are supposed to look after themselves.

I've admitted several times before that I wasn't right for the ministry, even when I had a modest faith that I don't have now. But in some ways I was only too glad to give the whole thing up. You can get so 'churchocentric' when you spend so much of your time there. It was only when I stopped going myself that I realised how much I'd expected the people to drop everything else in their lives and spend all their spare time with me on the 'sacred acre'. Meetings for this; committees for that, most of it just keeping ourselves going, not actually doing anything useful for anyone else. I didn't have time for a life outside so I didn't see why they should have one! Add in the joint efforts with other churches and it just snowballed. Success was always measured by how many turned up. Counting the sheep became a preoccupation – I only hope it kept them awake as well as me!

I would like to see a church that is much more blurred round the edges than focussed so much on its own members. Jesus certainly included some unlikely characters in his immediate circle. Fishermen (and shepherds incidentally) were often unable to keep up the religious rituals that good Jews were supposed to do because of their unsocial hours away from home. Levi was a tax-collector; Simon was a member of the Provisional Zealots. And, of course, there was Judas. Whatever his motive for betraying Jesus, and I personally think that 'Jesus Christ Superstar' got it about right by highlighting his disappointment with who Jesus turned out to be, he was still there until the very end.

There is a story in all three synoptic gospels about Jesus being pretty rude to his mother and brothers. (Yes, he did have brothers). They come looking for him, possibly because his behaviour was beginning to cause some embarrassment. He was probably not conforming to the proper expectations of his family, mixing with the wrong people etc. But Jesus points to his followers and says, 'These are my family now'. It sounds like the sort of thing a member of some cult might say to their anxious parents who have come to take them home, genuinely concerned for their welfare. But Jesus means the very opposite. He belongs to the people, not to any exclusive group – family, community or church. He belongs to the world; to the lost sheep.

So I guess that's where his followers should be today. I think I did see a sign outside a church once that said 'Trespassers will be welcomed', though it might just have been a recruitment drive. 'Trespassers' of course has a double meaning if you're familiar with the traditional version of the Lord's Prayer. I think Jesus was talking about a lifestyle that breaks out of our comfort zones and operates at the margins; not one that draws lines around 'me and mine' and keeps us safely within the fold. That might feel like security. Jesus' story seems to suggest that it is more like insecurity, at least as far as the Christian is concerned, because he is not there. He is out looking for the lost, not enjoying the cosy celebration back at the ranch, (to rather mix my metaphors)!

I cannot count myself among the sheep these days of course, but I too can try to make sure my life is lived in an inclusive way. Other organisations, institutions and lifestyles can be just as exclusive as the church can sometimes seem. 'Charity begins at home', and often stops there as well. To live a fully human life is to take on board the needs of others, not only of self. I often hear people say that they live as good a life as overtly religious people and I think they're probably right; and as bad a one as well! I am certain that you don't have to go to a church to live well. But not going doesn't automatically qualify you either.

There was a book once called 'Your God is too small'. That was about encouraging the faithful to get out more. My problem with the church is that their God is too big – too big an obstacle for me to belong. As a result I'm afraid He sometimes gets in the way of all the things we could still have in common, like making the world a better place by moving on to pastures new together.

7 Dealing with the debt – two parables about generosity

MATTHEW 18 VV.23-35; LUKE 7 VV.41-43

As someone interested in the dialogue between religious faith and our life in society, I couldn't resist this issue. I must be a useless dinner-party guest. Respectable people don't talk about religion or politics, and certainly not both at once as I'm about to. And of course the context within which I'm going to apply these stories isn't the same one as Jesus was thinking about – though there are some interesting parallels here and there.

Matthew's parable is a long story so I'll paraphrase. A servant owed his king a huge amount of money which he couldn't pay. It looked like his life was over so he begged his master to let him off and he did. But he then went out and bullied a fellow-servant who owed him just a few quid and refused to cancel his debt. The king, when he heard about it was not best pleased. He sent for the servant and this time he got his comeuppance! 'Let that be a lesson to you'.

This is one of those examples where the story immediately gets turned into an allegory about Jesus himself. Matthew sets it in the context of a dispute about forgiveness though this and the explanation at the end are probably not part of the original story. But the parable has usually been seen as talking about God's grace in dealing with our so-called sin. We have been let off a huge debt through the death of Jesus, (though that only works if you go along with the idea that I am lumbered with a great weight of sin just by being born). The King will not be impressed if we don't show how grateful we are, both to him and to other people. But forget that idea for a while and let's just treat it as a story about how human individuals and communities should behave towards each other. People who have been let off a big debt should not then go and persecute other people who owe much less.

So, to the politics. Dealing with the debt is the major economic and social issue of our time, so let's talk about it. Greedy financial institutions, here and in the USA, with the full knowledge of politicians who in many ways encouraged it, took a massive gamble and lost, because the people who then owed them money couldn't pay it back. There are signs that the whole global financial system may even be at risk – maybe endless economic growth is turning out not to be the rock that the west has assumed, though I doubt anyone would want to invest in 'Northern Sand'!

To save the banking and financial services industry from total collapse, we all had to chip in through our taxes to bail them out and write off their losses. As a result, the country now has to find the money to pay back the extra borrowing required, so family support workers, youth workers, education welfare officers and teaching assistants have become a luxury we can no longer 'afford'.

They will have to lose their jobs to try and put things right. Benefits will have to be cut and new schools not built. Somehow it's all our fault apparently. Public sector workers are a 'drain on the economy'. We will all have to work more, pay more and get less, except those who are still awarding themselves massive bonuses!

I'm not an economist of course, and no doubt it is much more complicated than that. But I wonder what Jesus would have had to say about all this? This is not a party political point because there's not that much difference between them. But I would like to live in a society that reduces inequality, not one where the powerless people have to pay while the bigger players carry on regardless. That at least seems to fit with Jesus' sense of natural justice in the way we should behave towards each other.

There's another story about debts in Luke; it might even have its roots in the same story. As I noted at the beginning, that often happens with the parables and is one reason why it's OK to create new meanings for new situations; it's been done before. In this story the amounts involved are much lower, though one is still much bigger than the other, and both servants get let off by the same money-lender. This time the point is about how the person who has been forgiven more will naturally show more gratitude – or not, as the case may be. It's much the same point. Those who have been given much are not then expected to be mealy-mouthed in return, but to be generous and treat others as they have been treated themselves.

The setting for the second story is the action of a woman, who we are specifically told 'lived a sinful life'. She poured a vast amount of expensive perfume over Jesus' feet while he was at the house of Simon the Pharisee. Jesus, generous to a tee, praises her. Simon is outraged. Prophets are not supposed to have anything to do with such people and I bet he was wondering where she got the money from. So Jesus tells the story and then again throws a question back at Simon. 'Which of those let off their debt should be the more grateful?' 'I suppose', says Simon, 'the one let off the most'. Right answer! 'So why criticise this woman's generosity?' The way we live should be a direct response to how much we have received. She had been forgiven much, so she gave much.

It is wrong that the burden of paying off the deficit seems to be falling most on 'ordinary working people' as the politicians like to call us, (though I think most of us are pretty extraordinary). I am sure that much of the pain of job losses and cuts to public services could have been avoided if we had wanted to do it some other way, like demanding more from those who can most afford to pay by way of windfall taxes etc. But, and take note of it, I also commend this government for sticking to its commitment to still increase overseas aid and development, despite the pressures here at home.

It would be even more unjust if we, the recipients of a standard of living that most of the world can only dream of, then became mean-spirited in response to needs that make our problems look like nothing at all. Getting rid of 'third-world' debt is one of the greatest moral priorities facing our world. For years the richer nations have made money out of the poorer ones, not the other way round. The amount they have to pay back bears no relation to what they have been given and simply keeps them in poverty. If we could cancel that burden this generation would indeed have something to be proud of.

But there are some hard lessons here about what we can reasonably expect for ourselves. There will be a cost to our generosity, or it won't be worth anything. The ungrateful servant, who wouldn't let go of what he was owed, should have seen that the cost to him was as nothing compared to the greater good that he had received. Simon the Pharisee should have seen that his own meanness held him back from seeing the example being set by the woman who may have been a sinner but could still teach him a thing or two. Jesus, as ever, seems to have got to the heart of the matter.

If we are to be more generous to those in far poorer countries than our own, as surely we must, then we shouldn't do it in ways that make the burden fall most on those who can least afford it. The rich, not the already-poor, should get poorer as a result. That's the decent way to do things which shows an appreciation of how much we have received. We have choices here and can make them in ways that seem consistent with natural justice, or not, as the case may be. I don't know whether this is stretching Jesus' stories too far – does it really matter? – but we are back to the parable of the talents again. More will be expected from those to whom more has been given. That seems only right and proper.

8 Issues of life and death –
The Last Judgement

MATTHEW 25 VV. 31-46

This is the last parable in Matthew's gospel, set just before Jesus' betrayal and arrest. The story of his life was coming to a climax and so no doubt it seemed to fit here in the context of the coming drama. Add to that the feeling that it was an apocalyptic age; everyone was expecting some kind of end-game in which God would intervene soon to save the Jewish nation from their oppression. Being in Jerusalem that Passovertime must have been like being in east Berlin just before the wall came down or waiting in Paris as the liberating forces grew ever closer in 1945.

Something big was about to happen, but would it work out for the best or was something even worse just around the corner? Judgement was on people's minds and Jesus was clearly understood, at least by Matthew, to be making some kind of claim about his own role in the anticipated crisis. Jesus uses the enigmatic title 'Son of Man' whose triumph is the catalyst for the moment of truth in the story. Does he mean himself or someone else? We don't know. This was probably just another Messianic title, but it seems to emphasise his solidarity with the people as the final countdown approached.

But the story Jesus tells again doesn't quite fit with what was expected. When the time comes, the King will divide everyone in all the nations, not just the Jews, (that's important) into two groups. Like a shepherd, he will separate the sheep from the goats. The 'righteous people' will inherit the kingdom and eternal life; the rest will be sent to eternal punishment. This was a relatively recent idea in Jewish theology and the religious elite, if not the ordinary people who were most attracted to Jesus, were pretty sure they knew who would be in each camp when the time came. This sense of our own eternal security has many echoes in those that I sometimes meet who are so sure of their own salvation that I have a strong urge to get this story out and make them read it!

For the people of the world are not divided along ethnic or religious lines. Issues of personal faith are entirely irrelevant. This is truly radical. It seems that the winners and the losers found themselves on completely different sides of the fence from what they had expected and, even more amazingly, they couldn't begin to work out why they had ended up where they did. It would be like a roomful of people standing in the throne room at Buckingham Palace waiting to receive a medal and asking each other, 'What did you do to be invited here'?, only to answer each other with 'No idea'. While another group of people were being carted off to the Tower without a clue about why they, of all people, had been chosen for such a fate. It's a very scary image. All the values and certainties that we thought we could live by are swept away on what appears, at first sight to be the whim of a powerful despot who is answerable to no-one. So what does matter in the end?

It was the things that were done, or not done, to comfort the poor, visit the prisoner, clothe the naked and support the stranger that had counted. It's the 'kingdom of God' on earth again. Those who were subject to the judgement apparently had no idea that it would be acts like these which would open or close the door to heaven. They had just done them because it was the right thing to do, or not done them. Only now was their significance made clear.

And this was the only thing that made a difference according to the story. No religion; no race; no sect, no individual was guaranteed to find their reward unless they had done what the King expected. Because in caring for those who were most vulnerable, the righteous had cared for him without knowing it. And in ignoring them, the rest had turned their back on the one they claimed to follow. It's an immensely powerful, world-shattering story that turns most ideas about religion completely on their head.

Now I don't of course believe in a literal final judgement of this kind. Life, for me, ends when I die just as it started when I was conceived. I was created out of nothing and to nothing I will return. But isn't the story actually about how we should live now, not a description of what will happen at some unspecified point thereafter? In truth, religious people have always been a bit confused about the timing of any such judgement, (whether straight after death or at some time later), because some, at least, have always found that it didn't happen when they thought it would. But the very idea makes no sense to me. I will live on for a while, I hope, in the minds and memories of those who have known and loved me. I hope I will be remembered for having lived life well, but that will be it.

Certainly the first Jewish Christians and many of those to whom Paul was writing a little later thought the end was nigh. But they were wrong. So was the evangelical preacher who predicted that the world would end about 6 months before I wrote this! It's easy to mock such mindless ignorance but the threat of a Final Judgement was a dominant force for centuries, graphically illustrated in most European Cathedrals and it still exercises a powerful hold over many. It's an idea we can well do without if it leads us to concentrate more on what will happen the other side of death at the expense of what we should be doing now.

Because surely the story can still help us to know what really counts in this life? It suggests that the heaven for which we may long, and the hell of which we may be afraid, are both possible, but only according to how we have responded to those who need us most. As I'm sure has been clear throughout, I have never been able to understand those who dismiss the 'social gospel' as somehow less significant than having a personal faith in your own salvation. Is religious faith just another kind of life insurance? What's commendable about that? It's not whether heaven or hell is waiting for me that matters; it's the heaven or hell that we have helped to create here and now. And there's not really any excuse for not knowing where our priorities should lie. For those who claim to follow him there is Jesus' story to show us, and, for the rest of us, our natural sense of what we know is right.

At the very least we need to have some idea of what life is like for those who are referred to in this version of the King's speech! This can be quite difficult. We increasingly seem to live our lives in silos that don't necessarily bring us into contact with the socially excluded and those on the margins of society. But any individual acts of kindness seem at least to count for something. My work has brought me into contact with people whose lives have been blighted by pressures that I have never had to face personally. I may have made a bit of a difference here and there, but not much. Perhaps I should pay more attention to the 'Big Issue' seller or the smelly guy with the dog on string.

But I know that's just scratching the surface. I personally know of great work being done to save lives and promote better childcare in the face of staggering poverty in Bangladesh. But then there's Africa, and so on and so on. It's overwhelming. Would any of us meet this standard if we have to? But there is surely a basis here for self-judgement, which is no bad way to live. At least let's make sure we don't see this challenge as somehow less important than the state of my so-called soul. Everything we do to make a difference to those who need it most is the most important thing we will ever do. We can never say we have done enough, but doing what we can is a test of our true humanity and I hope I never forget it.

9 'So who do you say I am?'

MARK 8 v.29; MATTHEW 16 v.15;
LUKE 9 v.20

I am close to the end of this particular journey; or at least a place to rest for a while, but there's a last-minute detour first. Each of these brief reflections so far has begun with a story Jesus told, or at least something he said, even if I have then gone off in some rather unconventional directions. But this time? Where's the story? PG Wodehouse had one of Bertie Wooster's friends say that a parable was one of those Bible stories that sounded at first like a jolly good yarn but which suddenly pops up and knocks you flat! I cannot sit down with my nice cold beer until I have come to a conclusion, not just about the stories, but about the story of the story-teller. The final parable is the one told about Jesus himself, so what do I have to say to him?

I have to conclude that he counts for something in my life or I wouldn't be writing this. Lest there be any misunderstanding, I am not abandoning my humanism or my atheism here. This is not a conversion on the road to Damascus or a dramatic *dénouement* where it all comes good in the final chapter and I find faith. There is no Being called 'God' who was at work in His Son Jesus to save me from my sins – there, I've said it again. The fatted calf is safe for a good while longer! But I have accepted that there was a man called Jesus of Nazareth; the evidence for him is as good if not better as for many individuals from ancient history. I have walked at least the second part of this journey in his company and he deserves an honest answer.

Jesus has often been seen as a 'paradigm' of human living at its best. There is a long tradition of 'The Imitation of Christ'. I too would hope to do the sorts of things in my life that Jesus did in his, as far as that is possible without a belief in his God. But at this distance I can only respond to the story told about him, not to him in person. I can't entirely separate his actual life from those who wrote about him; their version is all I have. John's gospel, for example, portrays Jesus as not just showing the way but as being 'The Way' in a much more exclusive sense. But doubt about the historical accuracy of John's account means these are unlikely to be Jesus' own words at the time. So I can't just take it all at face value.

This may sound like cherry-picking; only hearing Jesus when I want to listen to what he has to say! But I hope I choose with integrity. It's a story told by individual people, so I must take into account the insights of Biblical criticism about how and why they wrote it. This process need not undermine faith, as some have suggested, but is a rational and helpful tool in getting as close to the real Jesus as we possibly can. Surely it should therefore strengthen even those who have a conventional belief, because it also gets us closer to the truth? True faith cannot be built on misunderstandings and false assumptions.

But I can't entirely trust Jesus' subsequent followers to give me an accurate picture of his human life. As is evidently true with the reported lives of the early saints, there may be an element of 'bigging him up' to make the point. The nativity stories, for example, are clearly legendary and symbolic, designed to make links to Old Testament prophecy; they just don't add up as a factual record. Did the real Jesus actually walk on water and raise Lazarus from the dead? If so it seems odd that the earliest accounts left such dramatic events out, though even these claims have often been replicated by others elsewhere without leading to a new religion. An illusionist, whose name escapes me, walked across the Thames on my TV the other night. Clever and inexplicable, but I don't feel the need to rush out and hang on his every word as a result. There are several suggestions in the gospels that Jesus repeatedly tried to play down this kind of sensationalist view of him.

However, it seems that he was constantly interested in what people thought about him. Mark, for example, writes of repeated occasions on which Jesus had conversations about this with the disciples as they were walking along together. This seems to have been part of the process by which he worked out what his future would be, as well as going off into the desert. It's always good to combine time alone with time checking things out with others. Majority opinion among the people certainly appears to have been that Jesus stood in line with the prophets of the past. Some even seem to have believed that he was the Messiah, though there weren't many of them left once the going got tough. The religious leaders, of course, would have seen this idea as a threat so, given what happened to him in the end, this rings true.

I would like to live well and Jesus has been lurking in my background for almost 60 years. But given that I cannot attribute his life or death to the actions of a God who was behind it all, it seems I am still left with the two Jesuses with which I started; the Jesus of history and the Christ of faith. Is it possible to affirm the first but reject the second? – 'Christianity says no!'

The Creed in which I cannot join when I occasionally attend Evensong in my local Cathedral, says that 'for us (men) and for our salvation, he 'came down from heaven'; that he was 'born of the Virgin Mary' and that 'on the third day he rose again and ascended into heaven'. I can believe none of these as statements of fact about the historical Jesus, including of course the 'up and down' cosmology, though some would accept that it's not all meant to be understood literally. But it still doesn't make sense to me and raises far more questions than it answers.

More evangelical versions of Christian faith would place certain beliefs about Jesus absolutely at the centre. Not only did Jesus die and rise to some new kind of life again, but in doing so he took responsibility for dealing with the sins that prevent me from having a relationship with their God. If these sins are left unresolved by my lack of faith in him, God will still be cross with me when I die. To be fair, opinion varies widely about what will happen then, from graceful forgiveness to justified retribution. But these doctrines presuppose so many things which I just do not think are true.

But you don't really need to know anything at all about the life of Jesus in either of these understandings; it's only his death that is of significance. The concept of the kingdom, which he seems to have talked about continually, virtually disappears. His model of a human life well-lived is relatively unimportant. As these conversations in Mark suggest, Jesus did, it seems, sometimes talk of the idea that his death would make some kind of difference. But this is where it becomes more difficult to get back behind the church's version of him. They wrote the story about him; he did not write it himself. What did Jesus himself think it all meant?

He may have come to understand his death as some kind of self-sacrifice in the eyes of his God, but I really can't believe he thought it had anything to do with me two thousand years later. He almost certainly hoped that his death would usher in some new age which would deal with all the failures of the old religion of which he was so critical. Or, like millions of others, maybe he was unjustly put to death because he was a threat to those in power. Crucifixion was mostly used for those considered to be political prisoners. Pilate, we are told, had 'The King of the Jews' written above the cross, and would not be persuaded to change it. This all fits the Messianic context that has been evident all along. This has to be the answer to the question 'Why did Jesus die?' Whatever else might be seen as the meaning of his death, this was the actual reason. The rest, as they say, is history.

So does that make him just another failed prophet? Well, in a strictly historical sense yes, but the irony is that

I wouldn't even know about him had the Christ of faith not taken over. There have been many, too many, good people who have given their lives for what they believed in and whose names and deeds are now lost to us. I can find plenty to admire in the things Jesus apparently said and did, but he would be just another one had the story not gone on. It is only the fact that so many have subsequently believed in him, and in his God, that has made him stand out from the crowd. That is certainly a bit of a dilemma for me.

In his fantasy story 'The Good Man Jesus and the Scoundrel Christ', Philip Pullman explores this same issue in a different way. He imagines 'Jesus' and 'Christ' as twin brothers. It is Christ who chronicles the events of Jesus' life for later publication and who takes over from him after the crucifixion. Under the influence of a mysterious Greek 'angel', he is seduced by the idea of a future global church, rather than portraying Jesus' own emphasis on a Jewish sect which would otherwise have died out with him. The 'Christ' figure effectively betrays the Messianic 'Jesus' figure and then turns the story into something entirely different from what he had intended it to be. It's a clever idea, but without that realignment, would either of us still be writing about him today?

So what am I left with? Somehow, I have to leapfrog back over the church and consider my response to what I know of Jesus as he was. For me, Jesus of Nazareth is himself a parable; a real human man who demonstrated in his own life and teaching a way of living from which I certainly have something to learn. There is a kind of victory in his death, because the things he stood for still live on. He gave his life rather than compromise, and it was not all for nothing. A man of compassion and insight; a religious rebel, who wrestled with the best way to live and chose, not the easiest path, but the one that he believed was right for him to follow. A man who walked the same earth as I do and seems to have lived his life as I would like to live mine – a brother pilgrim along the way. A model for my own journey. But that's as far as I can go.

As I look forward to that cold beer, my final thoughts are suddenly of someone who was once my closest friend. He too was a minister for a short time; to my mind he was really good at it. He was a manual worker by background who related well to the people in the mining village where his church was; not a carpenter, but something similar. But it all went horribly wrong. One Sunday evening he went home after taking the service, told his wife he was leaving her there and then and that he'd been having an affair with a member of his congregation for months. He died of a heart attack only a short time later, still a young man. Some might say this was a judgement on him; to me it was just another human family tragedy and a sad loss to the church.

When we were both students, we were once asked how we would sum Jesus up if asked. The more pious members of the group came out with the usual statements about how he had died for their sins etc. I can't even remember what I said, so it must have been truly unremarkable! My friend, who later always considered his answer useless and embarrassing said, 'Good bloke. Bit of a lad. Left of centre. Liked a pint'. It may not quite get us to the heart of things but it's a start.

I will never be able to take on the idea that 'God sent us his Son'; those five words contain at least three impossible beliefs for me. But I am glad to have had Jesus of Nazareth's company on this journey. He has given me a great deal to think about. Perhaps we will meet up again on some future walk to continue the discussion. If not, the conversation has certainly been stimulating and maybe finding the way has become just a little easier as a result.

* * * * *

If you have got this far you deserve some kind of prize! I hope these two little books have encouraged some new thoughts in the reader, either alone or ideally in groups. As before, if you would like to respond to what I have written, please feel free to do so, as long as you can be charitable about it: ben.whitney1@btinternet.com. But I think it's goodnight from me, for now at least. I have some new, less self-conscious, journeys to make which will keep me busy for a while. This is it, so every moment counts, and I'm not remotely done with life just yet!